Awakening
Peace

Other Books by Darla Luz

The Heart of Attention

Free yourself from stress, and all inner conflict for good, creating a heart-felt life of perfection

I AM my True Self

Let go, feel free and awaken your dream life

Awakening
Peace

**A Step-by-Step Guide to Manifest the Life
You Want and the World You Want to See**

Darla Luz

Printed in the United States of America

ISBN Paperback: 978-1-7348913-4-8
ISBN eBook: 978-1-7348913-5-5

Book Cover and Interior design: Creative Publishing Book Design

Dedication

To my son, Brian, the miracle at birth who is awakening to his magnificence.

May you continue your highest path, being your true authentic self as you do the travel that you love and, as you've already realized that no matter how near or far our humanness is interconnected and one.

Wherever you go, my heart always follows.

And to my readers, my hope is that you realize in the pages of this book that we make life much more difficult than it needs to be

Table of Contents

Introduction   1

The Journey of Awakening   5

Chapter One: The Tools to Create the Life
    You've always Wanted   11
Tool #1 Intention   12
Tool #2 Breath   14
Tool #3 Peace   16
Tool #4 Imagination   18
Tool #5 Light   20
Tool #6 Awareness   24

Chapter Two: Loving and Appreciating Yourself   29
Remember only the positive   30
The path of growth begins with self-love, self-appreciation   30
Rephrasing negative thoughts   31

Chapter Three: Feeling Good   37
Be who you really are more often   38
Monitoring how you feel   40
Just as it is   42
Enhancing body, mind, and spirit   43
It is what it is   44
Becoming aware of the beauty all around you   47

Chapter Four: Living light   51

    Formless and selfless   55

    Know yourself as the radiant light that you are   57

Chapter Five: Creating your Future   59

    Thoughts create our reality   60

    Practice pure relaxation   61

Chapter Six: Manifesting the Life You've Always Wanted   63

    You are a co-creator with the universe   63

    Be the person that already has what you want   64

    Feel the excited emotion of what you want   65

    Stay in positive energies   65

    Become aware of signs, inspirational ideas, and insights   66

Chapter Seven: Letting Go of Negative Thinking   69

    Absolute belief and knowing must replace doubt   70

    You are not your negative thoughts   71

    You have everything within to create the life you want   72

    Things you want now come to you effortlessly   73

Chapter Eight: Awakening Peace in the World   77

    You are a powerful contributor to peace in the world   79

    You can create the world you want to see   82

    Awakening to your Magnificence   83

    Love is the highest vibrational energy   87

Easy Access to Practices   91

    Practice A Letting go and freeing yourself   92

    Practice B Dissolving inner conflict   93

    Practice C Merging your heart and mind   95

    Practice D Dissolving unwanted emotions   96

Practice E Touching others with light   97
Practice F Being Formless and selfless   98
Practice G Help manifest peace in the world   100

Can you please help?   101

About the Author   103

Introduction

This book was written for you, who wants peace, well-being, love, and joy in your life.

Whatever each of us want in our life, whether a car, a house, money, or a vacation, has within it a core reason, a true essence.

What we are really seeking is to feel at peace, loved, and happy!

Did you know that you don't have to wait for something great to happen in your life to make you happy?

You can feel happy now!

Within the pages of this book, you will learn to feel and make real the peace and joy that you may not realize is the true goal you have strived for all your life!

Did you know that if you feel the joy you would have if you already had what you wanted, you attract into life whatever you want more easily than if you just wished, craved, and yearned for it.

Those material things like a house or a car will now have a better chance of coming into your life and becoming real.

In fact, feeling peaceful moment by moment like feelings of love, Joy, and well-being will come very close to *guaranteeing* the manifestation of the life you've always wanted, even the life of your dreams!

Good news continues unlimited because, amazingly, the higher energies you are elevating through simply feeling good transforms every corner of your life and will now go out further and further to help alleviate a world of its problems! You, as part of an infinite whole, can help humanity to awaken!

You might be thinking that the world does not work that way.

I'm here to tell you that the technology of mobile phones, TVs, and computers we use daily and take for granted *does* work that way! We can hold in the palm of our hand virtually an infinity of information. We can see and hear through our devices, endless landscapes and people across the globe.

If you could have asked people that lived a hundred years ago if they could foresee and believe the technologies we have today, they too might answer: "*The world does not work that way!*"

The good news is each of us holds the same elements and energies that are within these amazing technologies. Then, why couldn't the energies within us work in just as an incredibly amazing way?

In between the pages of this book you are tapping into the incredibly amazing energies that are within you in this moment that can help you create the life you've always wanted. And they are instantly available, ready to be used *now*.

We are much more powerful than we believe!

We live in amazing times because humanity is more open and aware than ever of just how to tap into our power within to co-create with a vast and powerful Universal Life Force energy. In between the pages of this book, you will tap into that power.

How can I make such statements?

I study and research consciousness, and my passion is to expand the evolution of human consciousness in the world.

I am sharing with you here what I have learned, practiced, and now live bringing about many gifts and rewards in my life.

This is the third book I have written called the Heart Series of which *The Heart of Attention* is the first book. The second book is *I Am My True Self* which further expands on what I have learned and what I have experienced as I have journeyed through my path.

You are reading this, the third book where I expand even more on the infinite and joyous experience of self-realized, enlightened, and expansive growth.

Even if you have not read the first two books, you can still receive value by reading this book first.

In between the pages of this book, you are practicing living with more joy and a lot less struggle!

How you will be helped:

The moment you feel relaxed and peaceful, you are free, and you have let go of the useless, noisy mind of problems and worries.

You will *practice feeling the elevated feelings of* peace, joy, love, and well-being that are what you have been seeking all your life!

As you live in *elevated feelings, you attract better, elevated situations, circumstances, and relationships.*

You will experience self-love.

You will know the magical power of simply appreciating life that keeps giving you back what you are appreciating.

You will experience the power of imagining light that can, amazingly, dissolve for good all your worries and concerns.

You will discover the extraordinary power of your imagination that will help you manifest and create the life you want.

As you read through the book you will get a clear picture of how to maintain elevated states of life force energy on your path of awakening.

The practices you will be doing are an important part of your path. All practices within the chapters are also in the back of the book for easy access. At first you will read a practice as you do it, until you know it so well you don't need to read it anymore.

Are you ready to go beyond the rational, problem-seeking mind, silencing unwanted thoughts and emotions to create the life you've always wanted?

Are you ready to let go of sadness, doubt, self-criticism, stress, and fear?

Would you like to experience a life that fills you with excitement, vitality, and energy?

Turn the page and let's begin!

The Journey of Awakening

A s I look back at what I experienced that led to my path of awakening and the writing of three books, I am amazed at the depth of power hidden within each of us that seems to be a secret.

Yet the most beautiful event that is occurring today in a world that seems conflicted, difficult, and chaotic is that behind the scenes where it is not yet visibly obvious to us there is an awakening of the human spirit. And this includes *you* and I and every living being in the world!

The human collective is experiencing an innate desire to go towards more depth, more profound meaning than the gloom of wars, hatred, divisions, and barriers that has been endured for millennia.

Be assured that humanity is evolving and upgrading to a higher consciousness of peace, joy, wisdom and finally, love.

These higher energies of consciousness are indestructible, immeasurable and cannot be violated or destroyed.

Step by step, little by little there is an undeniable expansion and growth occurring within our collective spirit that will become more evident as humanity unites more and more in the beautiful energies of compassion, peace, joy, and love. These powerful, elevated energies being spread by our human collective are overcoming the weak, divisive, conflict-ridden low energies. And it is happening quickly!

The peace we greatly desire in the world will finally come about from the powerful reflection of our unified, interconnected peace within. And it only requires a fraction of the human collective to change the world!

You as an important part of the collective human family can help because every moment you practice being at peace, joyous, and kind increases the possibility of peace in the world. That is how powerful you are!

You will learn that in every moment you can choose to experience peaceful joy.

You might be wondering how you can experience peaceful joy when you are in the throes of stress, anxiety, fear, anger, and sadness.

In the pages of this book, you will let go and dissolve harmful energies that have caused you to suffer.

There is no fight, no battle, simply a relaxed inner peace as you practice taking deeper, comfortable breaths. This is how the mind of troublesome, harmful thoughts quiets down and dissolves. You now have space for peaceful joy.

And the more you practice, the more you open to your innermost self, the *genuine you* connected to an infinite Life Force and Source Energy that can change every corner of your life for the better.

I experienced stress, anxiety and fear when I faced the challenge of losing our family home that I wrote about in more depth in the first book of this series, *The Heart of Attention.*

It was one of those dark nights of the soul moments for me in which one is hopelessly lost in darkness, whether anxiety and stress or grief and heartache.

The way to transition from a perceived meaningless collapse in life is to seek shelter within. None of us are really equipped with the knowledge of how to find the haven, the sanctuary, and unconditional loving protection that exists in the depths of ourselves.

However, it is only there that we find the peaceful solace that is powerful beyond belief. Each of us has within us everything we need.

You will practice this peaceful solace here.

My hope is that you realize the great advantage of staying in these elevated energies because *being peaceful* is how you will effortlessly attract the life you've always wanted.

My journey is unfolding more and more miraculous and beautiful. I believe there is no destination, no journey's end on the path toward *a higher energy, Spirit, God, Christ Consciousness, Source,* whatever enlightenment is to you. Because it is infinite, limitless, and all-inclusive, no one is turned away.

The experience of joy, love, wisdom, compassion, and peace are each limitless and without end on the path of self-realization and enlightenment, available to every one of us despite what we believe or don't believe.

As a traveler on this path, I am not perfect! There *are* moments when I must extricate myself from past illusions. However, it is easier than ever to return to my peaceful self in an instant because I use the tools that I am giving you in this book. The peace, joy, love, fulfillment, and bliss are becoming more and more profound for me. So much so that I feel an increasing vibrational frequency that is pure bliss!

The more I experience these profound feelings, the less I experience and need to release past illusions, creating less and less struggle and much more joy in my life.

You deserve the peace, joy, and bliss that is available in every moment of your life.

What unfolds in life when we find our innermost peaceful self does not happen overnight. Until one day, as we look back, we can see clearly the perfect unfoldment of the big picture of our life.

What does happen quicker as we gain self-awareness, however, is an unfoldment in weeks or months, of synchronicities and serendipitous events that are truly miraculous! It happens when we continue going within with an aware, focused intention.

As you practice in this book, you will find the mind that once caused you great hardship now takes a back seat and allows you to be its master. Once you are the master, you will no longer need an outer world to bring you happiness. You will be free, and you will let go of the commotion of negative thoughts. And you will find within your innermost self the peace, joy, and vitality you deserve.

My hope is that you will know *who you are* by going within your silent, still spaciousness. I want you to notice how much better you feel as you focus on the positive, lightly and effortlessly. The life force energy that you will practice here is a driving force guiding me to write to let you, my reader, know the truth that exists within you. It is effortless and it is all within you, and every one of us, now, in this moment.

CHAPTER ONE

The Tools to Create the Life You've Always Wanted

The tools that you are learning to use here will bring about gifts and rewards in your life that are beyond anything you can imagine.

The tools within you now, at this moment, are ready to use and are unlike the physical tools used daily in our world to build, to create, and bring into form useful and often beautiful material objects.

The tools you are practicing here are not sharp-edged, heavy, or dangerous.

The tool kit you are about to learn here is *an experience of being light as a feather and free* because you have let go of the weight of baggage that crushes and depresses.

The crushingly depressive thoughts and emotions that circle over and over, keeping you stuck and trapped in a never-ending cycle of low energy, zapping your vitality and enthusiasm for life.

The tools that are within you are available now and have the capacity to change every corner of your life.

11

TOOL #1
Intention

Our intention creates our reality —Dr. Wayne Dyer

In the moment you decide to take a deliberate breath to a better feeling, you are putting into effect intention. While you may not feel anything of the great treasure trove you are activating within yourself in that moment, everything is real, and a lot more is happening than you realize because of your intention!

As you take a deeper breath feeling peaceful tranquility within, the intention you have is effortless. There is no need to use willpower to finally let go and feel free of endless unwanted thoughts and emotions. You simply feel the calming peacefulness within. The path to a higher level of consciousness is effortless, and intention will get you there.

You must remember that within you is a vast and beautiful power that can change your life. This power is there around the clock, always available in an instant. While it may be a bit challenging because we are all so distracted by what is going on in the outer world, practicing daily for a few weeks will help to develop the good habit of intention. It then becomes more and more effortless.

Keep in mind that when you have an intention to feel better you are opening a higher level of consciousness and you are well on your way to the dream that reflects the life you want. In the moment you deliberately take a deeper breath and relax you are intending to remove the blockages, the stress, anxiety, anger, and resentment we have all experienced that hinder us from moving forward in life.

Intention is guiding your energy in the direction of the life you want to experience. And you will realize that it is one of the most important things to do in any given moment. It is the starting point of creation. The important creation of the life you've always wanted!

Having intention is having a clear signpost of where you intend to direct your life. You know you want to feel the freedom of letting go of all that blocks you from the life you want, the energies of stress, anxiety, sadness, and anger. You are aiming to have an easier life lived with peace and joy and less struggle.

Just how do you incorporate intention into your everyday life?

A good way to incorporate intention is to cultivate presence moment by moment and, again, the easiest way to presence is being appreciative of all that surrounds you. You can be deliberate and have an intention to uplift your life force energy through feeling appreciative.

However, sincerity must be there! Because appreciation opens your heart and keeps you focused on positive thoughts. Remember when you are appreciative and grateful you are free, and you have let go of the noisy, disgruntled mind that is now silenced. You are no longer a victim of its relentless rantings. You are in full control and present in the moment, now.

Eckart Tolle, author of *The Power of Now* emphasizes, "The *now* is the most precious thing there is." When you have *presence*, you are no longer living in past sadness and resentment, nor are you living in future worry and fear.

As you practice intention, you have *presence now*, a powerful place to be. As you have an intention by taking a deeper breath you are in the present moment, which is your point of power, removing blockages, helping you open the door to the riches within you that can create the reality you want.

Intention at first may be a little challenging because you may forget to keep having the *intention* to purposefully shift to higher thoughts and feelings until you get used to a new daily routine.

Remember that much more is going on within than you may believe when you are purposefully taking deeper breaths and appreciating your surroundings! As you continue to practice, eventually your purposeful intention will become more natural, no longer will you need to do it on purpose. Remember that you are planting seeds that will sprout in weeks or months!

Intention is the dream, the vision, the goal of creating what you want in your life. Intention fits right into the practice of living consciously aware, opening your heart and loving life.

Keep in mind all the riches, the gifts and rewards you are opening as you have the intention to practice higher ways of being and thinking purposefully and deliberately.

TOOL#2
Breath

Your breath is the doorway to unimaginable gifts

When you take slightly deeper, comfortable breaths feeling relaxation and peace throughout your body, you open and become receptive to the energies that benefit not only your physical body but your entire life. It is as if you have opened the door to a sanctuary, a haven where you are protected from the chaos of an outer world. Once you are focused, the low energies of unwanted thoughts and emotions cannot enter this precious space within you.

Practice A

In the following practice you will experience your breath, the doorway into a spaciousness within that helps you let go and feel free.

Focusing on your breath to feel free and let go:

1. **Take several comfortable, even breaths giving attention to both your breath and the relaxed, calm feeling of your physical body.**
2. **Put your feet and legs in a comfortable position as you relax your thighs and your hips.**
3. **Focus on your stomach, your shoulders, and neck breathing smoothly and evenly, relaxing even further.**
4. **Continue with slightly deeper breaths as you relax your head, the muscles around your eyes, and your mouth, dropping your jaw just a little.**
5. **If your mind wanders, bring it back again and again to a focus on your breathing and a focus on the peace you feel in your physical body.**

Can you feel the peace and stillness as you relax your body, mind, and spirit?

You might think of your breath as a golden key that unlocks the door to many gifts and rewards in life.

This is the space from which you can release problems and concerns, and, if you want, ask for guidance, solutions, and answers. As you focus on your breath, you are going beyond your everyday mind to a space that is so powerful that what you need to better your life is known!

From this space you can connect with your soul, your higher self, spirit, or a higher power of your choosing. The more you connect to the spaciousness within you, the more true and real it becomes as it changes every aspect of your life for the better.

Our breath is one of the most important tools to change how we feel. Breath brings clarity to our thoughts, calming our emotions, bringing our mind and body to a restful ease.

When we are experiencing stress and trauma our breathing pauses and may stop in intervals altogether, so that our natural flow and harmony is lost.

Whenever you become aware of your mind complicating life and making things difficult, take a deep breath with attention and focus, and enter the peaceful spaciousness that will free you from all worry, anxiety and sadness.

TOOL #3
Peace

Inner peace is like the morning light that covers the darkness easily and effortlessly. —Darla luz

Inner peace is the gift that instantly frees you and allows you to let go.

Did you know that when you are at peace there is no fear, no worry, no anger, no unforgiveness; no harm to you mentally or emotionally. In the moment you capture a peaceful, relaxed feeling by taking a few deeper breaths, you dissolve an overwhelming thought and emotion whether it's stress, anxiety, or fear and worry.

We have all felt inner peace for moments in our lives, whether minutes or hours. We can recreate an experience of inner peace because we know how it feels, creating an asset of great magnitude on the path of awakening.

A feeling of inner peace comes from within so that you no longer rely on the outside world to bring you peace and tranquility. You now understand that only you can create inner peace that is available in any moment. And you are powerful because you are directing your life, no longer a victim of scattered thoughts and emotions causing overwhelm.

As you practice here to feel peaceful moment to moment you are detaching, giving less importance to stressful and anxious events. The peace you are activating is a safe and secure place improving your well-being because the stress and anxiety about events is slowly disappearing.

When you have inner peace in your life, your perspective of life changes, changing and improving what you experience through situations and relationships. The energy of inner peace affects an outer world, yet an outer world cannot affect your inner peace. The state of inner peace is powerful! You will experience events in your life that reflect the high vibrational energy of the inner peace you are feeling.

Inner peace is the gateway to a magical dimension filled with the wondrous miracles of an unlimited, abundant life. Its doorway opens simply as you learn to feel inner peace often through recreating it and resting in calming peace. It is possible to experience greater and greater peace, turning into a light-hearted, blissful feeling. As you cultivate, emanate and express peace, you no longer fight or battle anything or anyone and life becomes more effortless than ever. There is nothing to seek because you already *are*.

TOOL # 4
Imagination

As you imagine it, so are you creating it. —Sanaya Roman

It would be nice to know, wouldn't it, that if you intentionally imagine the future you want, that you are sure to get it.

What if I told you that if you imagine your future with *the same feeling you would have if you had it now*, and then let it go *knowing* it is on its way into your life, that it *will* manifest and become real in your life?

It may sound magical, but it's true!

When we imagine, we are free

When we imagine there are no limits to how much and how far our imagination can take us, the sky is the limit! This is what Einstein meant when he was quoted as saying, "Knowledge is limited *but imagination encircles the world."*

Knowledge can sometimes limit us when we are given a set of beliefs that most people around us take in as truth. An example is the belief that the world was flat in the Middle Ages. While seafaring nations in the world knew that the earth was probably spherical, those that held the "knowledge" that the earth was flat from the time they were born may not have wanted to deviate from the way of thinking of everyone around them, producing limitation in their lives.

Knowledge, however, is a good thing as humanity evolves in technology. It was knowledge that was needed to bring into form every material object in life. Every material object we see around us, whether a house, a skyscraper, car, plane, highway, table, or lamp was first seen in someone's imagination. The wherewithal, competence, and skill coming from knowledge was needed to build it.

Einstein also had in mind the mysterious force of our imagination when he was quoted as saying, "The most beautiful thing we can experience is the mysterious."

May you experience here the mysterious force of your imagination that can bring about the life you've always wanted. I experienced this mysterious force when I looked out at a beautiful lake and stood rapt in awe of its beauty. I had no idea whatsoever that I would be living in a house overlooking the exact shape and form of a lake which I committed to contemplating a few minutes a day, years before.

Even though I was not using my imagination but seeing the real thing, I've since learned that our subconscious mind does not differentiate between something real and something imagined.

So that we can imagine practicing playing the piano in our mind and being a better pianist, because our subconscious mind does not differentiate between physically playing the piano and imagining playing the piano in our mind.

For another example, once our nervous system knows the precise movement of shooting a basketball, we can imagine shooting a basketball in our mind, and the mind thinks that we have done it, because it doesn't differentiate between physically doing it and imagining it in our mind.

Does this open your eyes to how truly magical and powerful our imagination is! If we open to the tools available within us that can better our lives, we would be using a higher percentage of our mind and thereby open to many abilities and possibilities too!

Remember that as you imagine it, so are you creating it! I will repeat this several times throughout the book because that is how powerful and mysterious a force your imagination is!

TOOL # 5
Light

Our natural rhythm is to close our eyes to dark-ness and awaken to light. —Darla Luz

A quote from Einstein reveals the power of light: "Darkness does not exist. Darkness is the absence of light."

In everyday life, much time, effort, and importance are put into the darkness of life, the challenges and problems that seem to come at us in a never-ending chain of events.

Why do we allow darkness to depress our spirit?

Has staying in darkness ever brought us clear vision and foresight?

Has anything ever been solved through anger and worry?

Are we dwelling too long in the darkness of challenges that cause strife and confusion?

Doesn't the morning sunlight easily and effortlessly with no fight or battle overcome the darkness?

Observe as light allows the darkness to be exposed. Consider the many life forms that close, shut down, and withdraw in darkness, and watch as they open, enliven, and brighten in light. Humanity and many life forms are naturally attuned to sleep through the darkness of the night and awaken to a new day in light.

John Muir said it well: "wrongs of every sort are done in the darkness of ignorance ... for when the light comes, the heart of the people is always right."

You are practicing here to go towards the light when darkness is exposed. With no fight or battle you will simply allow the light to dissolve the darkness.

How did we lose the light we came in with at birth?

From the time we learned to live as part of society through our family, schools, teachers, the games we played, the movies we saw, and the news of the day we heard, we accepted that problems were a natural part of life. We were never taught that there was another, better way to live without the fear, stress, anger, and sadness that the darkness of problems produces.

Did you ever think there might be another way to live without feeling the difficult consequences of challenging problems?

Probably not because it is so ingrained in our earthly life that problems are a natural part of life, and we should just deal with them as best as we can.

The trait and characteristic of our temporary earthly experience, however, *is* about a continuation of naturally occurring problems! In our earthly experience everything seems separated, divided, and split. There seems to never be a coming together in harmony and accord to solve problems. So, problems and conflict continue in a never-ending, unresolved manner.

The good news is we *can* turn darkness into light.

Challenging problems are no longer there to trip us up, make us stumble and fall, unable to pick ourselves up.

Challenges are there so that we can grow and evolve as we learn from them! And the good news is, each of us can pick ourselves up on our own because we have all the tools within that are always available.

Albert Einstein said that he, as a scientist, enjoyed "the feeling of a rapturous amazement at the harmony of natural law."

We may not place enough importance on the amazing harmony of the natural law of the sun that our planet continually revolves around. Consider what would happen if the sun stopped rising and setting as it does day in and day out. Would all life cease to exist? The sun's light is life itself, and yes, life *would* cease to exist. Our life!

You might even include the word *love* when you think of how sunlight sustains and soothes all life through plants, minerals, and nature. Or how sunlight heals our body, mind, and spirit as it touches our skin, lifting depression and creating a path to joy. Or how we absorb sunlight into the many systems in our physical body, balancing, harmonizing, and maintaining our health and well-being.

Just as light heals us physically it should not be surprising that it can also heal our problems and challenges, transforming our experience of life for the better!

Light is one of the most powerful energies in the universe. As you imagine calling light to you, it is there in an instant ready to heal you mentally as it dissolves worries and concerns. You are practicing that here.

Remember that as you imagine it, so *are* you creating it!

You will dissolve any inner conflict with the vibrant, alive energy of light. The more that you call light to you, the more you will know and realize its power.

Practice B

All fear, tension, anger, and sadness, any inner conflict can vanish into nothingness as you imagine inner conflict dissolved in light. However, you need to be persistent in using light to dissolve thoughts. Because the more you fight, battle, and resist the low energies of unwanted thoughts, the stronger they become. So that as you *persistently imagine* dissolving thoughts easily and effortlessly with light, they will *exist only as light,* no longer harming you mentally and physically.

In the following practice imagine a powerful ray of light dissolving thoughts of worry, stress, tension, any inner conflict:

1. **Take several relaxing breaths until you feel peace and tranquility from your head to your toes.**

2. **Imagine a ray of light coming from a Universal sun that illuminates many worlds with its powerful rays. It is a golden light that cleanses and heals. Imagine it coming in through the top of your head.**

3. **As you take a comfortable breath in, allow the golden light to clear all energies in your body that cause you to suffer, holding your breath for a couple of seconds.**

4. **Then breathe out as if through a straw, slowly and comfortably, as you watch unwanted thoughts dissolve in light.**

5. **Continue breathing in the golden light and breathing out unwanted thoughts until you feel calm.**

Remember to be persistent in dissolving unwanted thoughts so that they *exist only as light.*

TOOL # 6
Awareness

*Awareness of ourselves within leads to the change
we have always wanted.* —Darla Luz

Awareness of something that is delightful and pleasant that helps you get out of bed in the morning is always reflective of something you love. That alone gives you the life force energy that flows in the direction of the kind of life you want. You are activating enjoyment, enthusiasm, and vitality for life, and you are free from anything that might keep you from ascending the upward spiral of higher consciousness, which is one of the most important things to do in life.

What is enjoyable, delightful, and pleasant to you can be as simple as learning something new. Perhaps you want to travel, learn a new language, improve skills in a musical instrument, spend time with a loved one, or you are pleased and excited to care for a pet or a garden.

Remember that our lives change for the better when we are no longer in the darkness of unwanted thoughts and emotions. And, instead, very much aware of ourselves and our surroundings.

You will realize and understand that the aware focus within you is now on higher energies that serve you, rather than the low energies that are detrimental and are no longer useful to you. Things that just happen in your daily life are now reflective of the clear, focused *life force energy* you are putting into the world.

Today, in daily life most of humanity's focus is on eighty per cent or so of the outer world's divisive actions. Without aware focus on something meaningful in our lives we indulge in varying degrees on anything that grabs our interest and causes our minds to become scattered and strewn about without purpose.

When you are focused on something exciting and meaningful, you have awareness, and you have purpose. Being excited about something does not have to be spiritual in nature. Perhaps you found a new recipe you'd like to try or a new program you'd like to watch. When you feel excited and enthusiastic about something, you are also acknowledging a means to who you really are, what you love to do, your true nature, your genuine true self and spirit.

This alone is expanding your consciousness into a higher consciousness.

Remember that awareness of what you think, say, and do daily is crucial. Only when you have awareness can you then have the intention to practice the tools you are being given in this book.

Having awareness is not as difficult as you might think. There are many doorways to awareness. One of the easiest is to practice appreciation and gratitude as you look around at your surroundings. In those moments you are in a life force energy taking you in the direction of the life you've always wanted. You have opened your heart and become receptive to whatever you appreciate, and the universe gives you more of the same.

Another way to open to awareness is to focus on your five senses, allowing you to become vibrantly alive in the present moment.

A meditative practice that will help train your mind to focus on the present moment has always been and will always be a path to higher consciousness. An easy meditative practice for me was contemplating a calming and beautiful nature scene.

When feeling overwhelmed, we can take a deeper, easier breath, become aware, and do something that we enjoy. Going out into nature is a great way to recover and put our mind at ease. Watching the playful antics of a pet or a child rejuvenates our spirit. As we take our mind from what makes us feel overwhelmed, we can come back to an experience of the pressures of an outer world with a calmer and more relaxed and peaceful attitude. A relaxed and peaceful mind in higher consciousness is much better at coming to grips with what may seem like problematic situations. Thinking in higher ways leads to solving problems more easily through a wiser mind.

When we tap into the higher life force energy of something we enjoy, we are in that moment *aware*, and we access the higher mind of consciousness. Remember awareness *is* consciousness!

Awareness of yourself is key to seeing change in yourself. An awareness of maintaining a high energy life force through something you love to do is a means to self-awareness and realizing your identity, who you really are! You were never the person living in the past in anger, frustration, and regret. Nor were you ever the person living in future fear, anxiety, and worry. You are your true self, genuinely living now in this moment in vibrant aliveness because your thoughts and emotions are on what you truly love.

As we live in awareness guarding and experiencing our peaceful and joyous inner being, we realize and understand that challenges are only there to help us evolve and grow in our view and perspective of the world. Living in peaceful joy with a better outlook on life creates no limit to how far we can evolve.

The good news is that we can choose the life force energies that make us feel better in any given moment and that we can maintain moment by moment.

This is how you become the change you want to see in the outer world.

Everything must first change within your Self before you see change in the outside world. Ghandi's words, said almost a century ago, is as true today as ever, "**Be** the change you want to see in the world."

It is just as true to "*Be* the change you want to see in your personal life."

As you progress here, you will understand that *awareness moment by moment* is the key to a changed personal life.

There is no limitation to what you receive when you have awareness within. And that includes not only the things you want in your life but also your gifts and abilities.

And the proof that what you can have in your life is limitless is in the projection of what your consciousness has already manifested in your life.

What do you think of your life now?

Remember we create our life. It is molded through how we feel, what we think, and do.

A way to improve on what you see is to be aware of the vibration you are holding because that is the vibration you attract! Or put another way, everything is energy. A high vibration and frequency of higher thoughts and emotions will attract the same.

So that when you feel excitement and enthusiasm for life, that is what you will experience. The energies of excitement and enthusiasm will bring about situations that give you the same.

The *awareness (consciousness)* you are experiencing here is a fundamental part of attracting beautiful experiences in every corner of life. As you practice experiencing higher energies in pure awareness, those situations that once bothered you will no longer concern you. You now live through the peace, joy, and unconditional love you feel

CHAPTER TWO

Loving and Appreciating Yourself

You may have heard that you cannot love another if you don't love yourself first. While it's true, just how do you learn to love yourself?

An easy way to learn to love yourself is through appreciation. Appreciate yourself for how far you have come on your path of growth through the many setbacks and challenges you have faced. Have compassion, which is a close link to love, for the way you handled each challenge in the best way you knew how.

Appreciation is a link to the heart, opening it so that the energy of appreciation heals the heart physically, lowering blood pressure and reducing the risk of heart disease. All areas of life are influenced as our heart opens through appreciation and gratitude. The increased positivity and feelings of love that appreciation and gratitude give us help relationships flourish, lifting our spirits. Our elevated thoughts and emotions reach out into all areas of our life.

Remember only the positive

Can you think of a moment in life that made you proud of something you said or did? Perhaps, you stood up for someone when you saw them being treated unfairly. Or maybe you showed someone support that they noticed and then thanked you.

Think of a moment when you gave someone a few words of encouragement.

Consider all those moments when you received praise and were honored for diligence and hard work. There are many more moments in which you can congratulate and feel good about yourself than you may realize.

Be playful and creative in the way you remember these moments. You might imagine each in beautiful golden hues so that they become extraordinary memories in your mind. Imagine them often. And allow good, true thoughts about yourself to take precedence over false thoughts and feelings about yourself. Understand that the ordinary, everyday mind produces endless false thoughts.

Always remember that you are perfect just as you are!

The good news is that when we appreciate who we are the mind of problems and concerns quiets down. This rational mind begins to recognize, more and more, our true significance, merit, and value.

The path of growth begins with self-love, self-appreciation

Unloving thoughts that tell us that we are not good enough, that we cannot succeed, that we are too this or too that come through the false mind less and less, losing steam and becoming weaker and weaker. The more we appreciate who we are, the more the chain of low energy, unwanted thoughts that make us feel bad, and the emotional hardship they produce, is broken. We are little by little becoming less and less stuck and trapped in hopeless despair.

Sometimes we become unconscious and cannot hear the thoughts that belittle, berate and depress us. It is important to stop and ask ourselves why we feel down. What, exactly, did the mind of problems tell us when we were unconscious?

The ordinary mind of problems can be unbelievably cruel. Thoughts come through our mind that we would never think or say aloud in conscious awareness to a friend or a loved one. It is obvious, isn't it, that when we are in the grip of the negative, everyday mind we do not love ourselves!

Keep in mind that eighty per cent or more of thoughts coming from the everyday mind are negative and recycled repeatedly. The same thoughts we had yesterday and the day before, and sometimes months and years before, are the same unwanted thoughts causing suffering and hardship. You are practicing here to replace the thoughts that harm with better, higher energy thoughts that benefit your health, well-being, and vitality for life.

What triggers a feeling that brings us down? Is it the social media picture reminding us we must look more fit and trim? Is it the picture of the car and the wardrobe we want that we think we will never have?

Rephrasing negative thoughts

Be purposeful and deliberate in the way you create a better feeling, relieving your mental and emotional health. Begin affirming out loud or to yourself the opposite of those thoughts and feelings that bring you down, that make you feel hopelessly depressed.

Now, 'I will never be fit and trim,' turns into 'I am seeing results in weeks because I am eating better and exercising.'

Now 'I will never have the car or the wardrobe I want,' turns into 'I am earning more money from what I love to do.' Or 'I am abundant. Everything I want comes easily to me.'

Repeat affirmed statements called affirmations and give them the power to manifest and become real in your life.

One way to make your affirmations more powerful is to say them with conviction and a *knowing* that they in fact are real and true. It is alright if you don't believe them at first because when you say them with conviction and belief, your subconscious mind will take them in as truth the more you repeat them. The subconscious mind is powerful and will bring into your reality what you know to be true and believe!

A good time to verbalize affirmations is in the morning just as you awaken or just before you fall asleep. This is what is called your alpha state in which your subconscious is more receptive, open, and creative.

The subconscious mind does not know the difference between a statement, a thought, or something imagined that has happened and one that has not yet happened. It takes in all thoughts that you speak and think, and whatever you imagine as real and true.

That's why it's important to be positive and never negative when you make statements about your life. When you begin an affirmation with, 'I *Am…*' and say it with conviction you are emphasizing it, making it clearer and more definite. This definite clarity will allow it to become real and manifest even more quickly into your life. '*I Am …*' also taps into the infinite space of potentialities and possibilities that you are joining and becoming more a part of here. '*I Am …*' said with conviction is who you are and what you experience and opens you to Creation Itself.

As you open your heart and appreciate who you are and how far you have come on your path, you will radiate the energetic feeling of love to all life around you, including those you love, pets, and all of nature.

Keep in mind that as you simply *feel good* you are already aligned to bring about the life you want.

You will realize just how simple it is to open your heart. Simply focusing and imagining light in the area around your physical heart does much more than you know. This simple gesture helps your physical brain by improving its circuitry in ways that are beneficial to your body, mind, and spirit.

According to Neuroscientist and author of *Becoming Supernatural*, Dr. Joe Dispenza says that when we focus on our heart, we elevate feelings of love, joy, peace, creativity, and inspiration. And as we sustain these feelings, the brain and the heart become cohesive, balanced and in harmony as one.

Practice C

In the following practice, your brain is absorbing the good and pure qualities of the heart.

Take slightly deeper, relaxing breaths so that you feel peaceful serene tranquility that extends from the top of your head to your toes. Continue until you feel completely relaxed. Put focused awareness on the area of your heart, imagining light pouring out from it. Imagine a stream of light coming from your heart extending upward to your mind and back downward to your heart. As you relax more deeply, imagine the stream of light extending upward, then downward to your heart again and again. Stay here as long as you like, feeling the peaceful tranquility and cohesion of your heart and mind, in harmony as one.

As you continue to focus on your heart, the energy field of love expands reaching all areas of your body, and out further and further, creating a sphere of light, reaching everyone and all life around you and beyond.

Remember that you have let go and are free as you revel in the peace and tranquility of an open heart, and you are perfect just as you are. As you are peaceful in this elevated state, you are in the elevated feelings of love, joy, creativity, and inspired thoughts.

Keep in mind that appreciation is a link to our heart and opens us to love. When we appreciate, whether ourselves, our physical body, people, our surroundings, the food we eat, what we see, do, and hear, we naturally express the energy of love.

Think about how perfect you really are.

You are replacing positive, good, peaceful, joyful, and true thoughts about yourself rather than thoughts that are often self-deprecating, inadequate, and false.

From this moment on, if you have a thought that does not make you feel good, put light around the thought and watch it dissolve in brilliant light that is sparkling and shimmering. Or you might imagine the thought moving through the sky like a cloud dissolving and clearing a sunny blue sky. You are dissolving unwanted thoughts in a gentle, non-judgmental way through your imagination. There is no fight or battle, and no low energy emotion that produces hardship within. You are the master of your life! No longer feeling diminished or victimized.

Remember, your imagination is powerful!

When you are in the energy field of love, focusing and linking with your heart as you appreciate, send a negative thought the light that represents love. Or simply say "I love you" and watch it disappear.

The energy field of love is powerful!

One very profound reason to love yourself is because you have the eternal and the infinite inside of you. And *that* can move mountains!

So, you see, reaching the rich spaciousness within you from where you can create better circumstances, situations, and relationships *does* begin with changing yourself. However, you may have already noticed as you have practiced, changing your personality does not have to be an uphill battle you have to climb in blood, sweat, and tears. It can begin with focusing on what you love, remembering good, positive experiences, and affirming good, true beliefs about yourself.

CHAPTER THREE

Feeling Good

*You don't have to wait to feel good, you can
feel good right now.* —Darla Luz

Y ou don't have to wait for something in the outer world to
make you feel good. Remember that you are the master of
your life and have full control of what you are feeling at every
moment, no longer influenced by an outer world. You are aligned
with a universal flow that is infinite, everlasting, non-wavering,
and constant. And when you are aligned, you are like a magnet
that attracts good things into your life.

Things that happen outside of us, in the outer world, always
begin and then end. It is a trait of our human existence on this
earth planet. Perhaps we experienced looking through rose-colored
glasses at a new relationship, in which everything seemed perfect,
only to find flaws a short time later. Or maybe we got the position we've been wanting, only to feel stressed and anxious with
more responsibilities. Notice that whatever situation or event
that brings you excitement and happiness in the outer world
spikes up then as if by the law of natural gravity comes down.

When we wait and rely on events that happen in the outer world to make us happy, feel-good energy goes off the chart, spikes up abnormally high, only to experience a spike down a short time later to the same degree that it went up. It is not in the natural flow.

We are no longer living in the natural, balanced, flow that gives us a spectrum of ease, love, peace, joy, bliss, and fulfillment. These are the qualities we can experience when we live in *presence, now,* focused and aware of a good feeling.

It is always important to be aware of how we feel. Think of a feeling that brings you down as an indicator, a friend, letting you know that you are not moving forward in life because you have lost the elevated good feeling.

You can feel good right now as you relax, breathe a little deeper and take in the wonder and awe of life; the natural world and all life forms, even if they are only in your imagination.

Remember that feeling appreciation and gratitude is the easiest way to a good feeling. All too often we rely on the outside world to bring us "happiness." We can create an elevated good feeling on our own without relying on the outer world.

However, you are opening to so much more than simply a good feeling! Your everyday mind cannot even fathom the possibilities that are in store for you as you cultivate feeling good moment by moment.

Be who you really are more often

It is important to be who you really are more and more often. The *you* that is revitalized, regenerated, and enthused about life. The *you* that lives in the present moment, mastering your life, no longer victimized by false narratives coming from a false mind.

How might you use this moment to expand your consciousness, going beyond the mind that all too often blocks you from creating a life that is joyous, peaceful, and filled with the energy of love.

The path of self-awareness, self-realization, and enlightenment is one of joy, enthusiasm, and unconditional love; doing what you love to do, loving all life, including those that you once held resentment toward. This is the path available to each one of us because, in truth, we are all connected and one with Source Energy, the infinite spaciousness within.

In fact, the more you express who you really are, wise and aware, the easier it is to shift quickly from lower energies to higher energies that benefit you, because your mind is so clear and your awareness more prominent than ever. Wisdom and awareness come from realizing what is important in life, the joy, peace, and vitality you feel.

Rising above and going beyond the everyday mind and the outer world is not just a means to escape the confusion and chaos of everyday life. Rising and going beyond entails going toward the energies that are a part of who you are, a creator who can carve out the experiences of the life you want.

When you get up in the morning enthused and revitalized because of something that moves you, something you have an aware focus on, you are on a path to create the life you want and to help create a better world too! More will be said in the chapter called "Awakening Peace in the World" about how each of us can help direct humanity toward peace through the powerful energies of awareness, appreciation, and simply feeling good, all of which we are cultivating day in and day out and moment by moment.

Monitoring how you feel

Considering all that is in store for us as we cultivate feeling good, it becomes crucial to often monitor how we feel throughout the day.

As you finish a task and before you start another, sit and monitor how you feel.

Probably the number one and most important thing to write on our to-do list is what we are thinking and feeling as we go about our day. In fact, that should be a top priority.

Because once we deliberately and purposefully feel a better mood, and are no longer harboring thoughts and emotions of anger, regret, and judgement, absolutely everything gets done easily and effortlessly, without anger or resentment.

It does take time and effort to keep monitoring our feelings. However, as we do, we are paid back in infinite ways. And staying stuck in feelings and emotions that bring us down is simply not worth the pain and suffering that these low energies reflect into all areas of life.

As you sit and monitor how you feel, use your breath as the tool that can help you relax. Remember that the focus you have on your breath quiets the mind of chatter. If the mind interferes with your focus on your breath, bring focus back again and again to your breath.

There is much more happening than you realize as you bring your focus back again and again to your breath. You are training your mind to connect and become affixed to the present moment. Keep in mind that as you live more and more present and aware, you are relieved of past sadness and future worry.

If you experience a mood that brings you down, you may want to consider the chain of thoughts that brought your mood down, without dwelling on them. In this way, you are becoming aware. Having awareness is the goal because you are being your Self in consciousness the moment you are aware. You are ascending the upward spiral of a higher consciousness as you gain awareness, which *is* consciousness.

The good news is the more you cultivate and nurture feeling good, the clearer your mind because unwanted thoughts come through less and less. You are becoming more easily aware of the chain of thoughts that brought you down.

Are you feeling strong emotions that seem to persist? Perhaps you are feeling a strong emotion coming from recycling unwanted thoughts that get stronger as the thoughts recycle again and again. Allowing these types of thoughts to stay and increase aggravating emotions can lead to hours, weeks and even months of experiencing sadness and disillusionment. It is not uncommon for depression to then fester for a lifetime, potentially causing a variety of diseases.

Practice D

In the following practice, you are allowing a strong emotion to pass through you with no fight or battle:

**Allow a low feeling of sadness, tension,
or anger to pass through you
Take several deep, relaxing breaths and allow the
feeling, not the thought, of a strong emotion to pass
through the area of your heart. Feel the energy of**

the emotion no matter how intense. It is alright if you tear up, it is simply the strength of the emotion making its way through you. Imagine the emotion turning into light, dissolving within you. Continue focusing on the light within you as you take slightly deeper breaths feeling the serene tranquility of peace and calm. And imagine the light within you increasing in power and strength.

Eventually these strong emotional energies will subside, dissolving altogether, never to bother you again so that you can feel the freedom and the letting go.

Remember to think of the unwanted thought for just seconds, allowing only the energy of the emotion to pass through you. Allowing only the energy of the emotion that is causing inner conflict to pass through you, feeling its energy each time, will eventually lose its power over you, subside and vanish altogether.

Remember that when you resist by fighting and battling emotions like anger, sadness, regret, or fear, they will persist. There is no fight or flight as you allow an emotion in peaceful awareness. Accept, allow and imagine the emotion turning into light as it passes through you.

Just as it is

Doing this practice, each time a strong emotion is taking you over will, more and more, benefit you because you are experiencing acceptance. Accepting everything just as it is gives you a serene feeling. You no longer fight or battle unwanted thoughts and emotions. You are free and you have let go.

Do this practice each time you feel a strong emotional charge coming from unwanted thoughts.

Allowing and feeling emotions is how you move through them. As infants and young children, we were resilient, crying over a taken away toy, then, in the same moment, laughing through our tears through an awareness of something funny. Slowly, but surely, we learned to obsess over, hold on to, and try to resist unwanted thoughts and emotions, making life difficult.

Remember, you have a choice. As you accept an emotional feeling and turn it into light, you are choosing the higher peaceful feeling of freedom and letting go.

The good news is that shifting to feeling good, whether it's serene peace or enthusiasm, will naturally form a habit, helping you aim for a higher, lighter, better feeling more and more often. As you do, you are seeding seeds that will sprout what will seem like little miracles in weeks or months!

Enhancing body, mind, and spirit

As you feel lighter in spirit, joyful, and at peace, you help the natural flow of your physical body; its ability to continually maintain itself without your involvement and effort. The endless processes needed to *sustain our physical well-being are more and more understood by science. However, our amazing physiology is becoming more mind-boggling and mysterious!*

In the same way that you do not need to control the inner workings of your physical body, the peaceful feelings you are purposefully cultivating will now relieve your mind and create more ease and less struggle in your life, without a need to control worries or concerns.

The inner workings of your physical body are influenced as all parts are taking on the higher frequency and vibration that come from feeling more joy, peace, and well-being. The cells and atoms are taking on the higher vibration of the energy field of love coming from your heart-felt feelings. Appreciate cells and atoms for the job they are doing to maintain your physical body without you having to control the endless systems working around the clock on your behalf. Your cells and atoms will now do a better job as you as their master appreciates them!

We may go about our day never considering just how our physical body works without our need to control it. It is astonishing when we hear about the thousands of miles of blood vessels that make up capillaries, arteries, and veins that constantly work around the clock. Imagine having to control every system, every organ in our physical body all day long.

Would we pay as much attention to the concerns and worries, the situations and circumstances, that take up space in our mind if we had to control the continuous, strategic forces going on in our physical body? This realization gives insight as to how truly wasteful daily attention on worries and concerns is.

Doesn't it make sense to begin our day with an appreciative good feeling for the very alive systems within that continue uninterrupted throughout our lives? Appreciating, honoring, and being grateful for our physical body leads us to a higher life force energy and increases the nurturing of self-love.

It is what it is

Remember that everything that you experience is perfect because you are getting back the exact energy you are putting out. It is important to remember that through the positive energy we are putting out into the world, we are receiving exactly the energy needed for us to evolve, grow, and expand into a higher, finer consciousness.

Even as you practice a higher, better feeling, if what you see in life is not what you want, know that situations that have needed remedying are now coming to the surface to be remedied once and for all. They are there for you to grow and learn from.

Understand that trying to snuff out or battle a situation that may not be to your liking is not the answer. Stay in the energy of a good feeling and the situation will weaken and dissolve as all negative situations eventually do. Challenging situations are always temporary and fleeting in our third-dimensional life. They are weak, have no staying power, and can be dissolved with a higher energy of light and vibration.

Embrace and accept challenges for being the signposts that help you and all life around you grow. Embracing and accepting everything you see, without labeling or judging the energy is what is meant by allowing the moment to be just as it is. As you accept situations and circumstances, there is less struggle and more ease in your life! You are serene as you simply *observe* what happens in the outer world, without getting *absorbed* in it.

The energy of observation is powerful and is backed by science. An object that observes a subject creates change in both. So that as you observe a situation, not getting involved in it, it changes both you and the situation.

You may be asked for your opinion about a challenging situation. Your opinion is valuable because you are observing and witnessing from a higher mind of wisdom and discernment.

However, if you are tempted to try to control a situation involving a friend or loved one, remember we are all here to learn from challenges and each of us has an inner knowing about how to handle our own challenges.

Keep in mind that the highest vibrational energy within you always wins out, despite what is going on in the outer world! The high vibrational energy of peace and joy you maintain moment by moment magnetizes the same high vibration through the matching, harmonizing energies of synchronicities. So that as you maintain a high energetic vibration everything that happens to you takes on the higher vibration of flourishing relationships and improved situations and circumstances. An especially high energy of simply feeling good weakens and dissolves fleeting negativity quickly.

When you are enthused, joyous, and at peace, you are whole and complete, focused on the high energies of light and vibration. Keep in mind that is what reflects into your life.

The higher energies you are activating through feeling good are infinite and unlimited! Surrender and feel at peace with daily situations in life. Allow yourself to feel the serene peace.

Look at what surrounds you and *be* in harmony with what you see in this beautiful earth existence that makes you feel good.

Feel the feeling as you look at a glistening night sky or a full golden moon. There are endless things to feel in this world and they could all be positive, helpful, upbeat, and encouraging. Feel the music, the song whose vibration and frequency match your inner harmony, always aligning you with the best that life has to offer.

Are there people, places, animals, or nature scenes that you love? Is there something that puts a smile on your face as you think about it? Turning away quickly from focusing on the low energies of boredom, sadness, disheartenment, or anger, accelerates your path of awakening, greatly improving all areas of life. Practice moving into and shifting to a better feeling moment by moment!

Becoming aware of the beauty all around you

You may find beauty in the most unlikely places.

My father was someone who was always genuinely positive and easy-going, radiating a light-hearted energy that made others feel comfortable to be around him. Growing up, my friends and acquaintances described him as "cool, nice, and great."

You too may be someone that naturally resonates with an elevated life force energy that is inherently ingrained in the human spirit. Some of us must be more deliberate and purposeful in reaching this higher level of consciousness. The good news is you are practicing it here.

As my father's health declined, a doctor's visit, though he never said it, was not something he looked forward to.

On one doctor's visit as I looked for a parking spot, present and appreciative in the moment as was my father's nature, he noticed a hedge, its leaves turning into the orange red hues of autumn, momentarily lifting his spirit. Looking up at a bright blue sky he commented on the "beautiful morning," helping him further maintain a higher energetic spirit. He was being very general in his appreciation of life. He merged an awareness of the natural world with his personal experience at that moment. He then took a deep breath focusing upward, holding the higher vibrational good feeling, noticing that the people around him in the waiting room, the nurses and the doctor, everyone, responded in kind, creating a better, feel-good experience for his doctor visit.

As I write about elevated consciousness today, I can see clearly my father's natural inclination to be his Greater version and higher, true self.

In every moment, each of us can find that higher vibrational feeling.

Esther Hicks, author of *The Law of Attraction* and *Ask, and It is Given*, encourages a general appreciation and gratitude of life when in a moment that seems overwhelming, we don't quite know where to turn.

Looking up, instead of being amid a polarized, dualistic world is helpful. You are the clear sky behind the stormy clouds. If you can't see beyond a cloudy sky, close your eyes and imagine a sunlit, clear blue sky. If you are in hopeless despair about a situation in your life, be very general about what you appreciate and are grateful for. Keep that high vibration as you commune with nature; perhaps walking through a park, hear the gentle rustling of leaves on a tree, the sunlight coming through the trees, creating images of leaves on the grass. Open your five senses to the beauty all around you.

Remember to affirm when you wake up in the morning everything that is truth about you. Shift the narrative of the everyday mind. Now "I will never succeed" turns into "I am successful." And "I'll never find my soul mate" turns into "I *am* special, and I *am* attracting someone special."

Use your imagination and picture the kind of life you want. As you are picturing it, feel how you would feel as if you had it now. Feel the joy, the enthusiasm, and the exhilaration.

Know without a shadow of a doubt that what you picture in your mind, what you are imagining, is on its way in this moment, because it *is*. Because it is on its way, be grateful and appreciative by repeating "thank you," "thank you," "thank you," with meaning.

If doubt comes into your mind, put light around the negative thoughts that tell you that it can't happen. Or turn away from thoughts that are not true in the many ways you have learned in this book. You might imagine unwanted thoughts like clouds and watch them disappear as they clear a blue sky. Or you might imagine brushing them away gently with a feather.

Remember that the high vibration of joy, enthusiasm, and exhilaration you are feeling is a match and in harmony with the kind of life you are imagining. For this reason, it is crucial that you maintain a high vibration. *Know* that what you are imagining is on its way!

Keep in mind that negative situations in life are temporary. They don't have staying power. You have the infinite and the eternal within you and you are powerful.

However, there are times in which life takes an unexpected, difficult turn. Are you experiencing a situation or circumstance in your life that seems hopeless?

Perhaps there has been a job loss, a separation from a loved one, or simply stress, tension, and despair that doesn't seem to go away.

Remember to appreciate very generally as you look up and away from being amid difficulties. There are beautiful things to appreciate in this world! And a deeper, calming breath is one of them!

Remember that the journey toward enlightened self-realization is an upward spiral that pauses and slows as we grow through challenges and then continues its movement upward toward higher consciousness.

CHAPTER FOUR

Living Light

Awaken to the light that heals all life. —Darla luz

As we know ourselves as an infinite, eternal life force of pure energetic light, we benefit greatly. And as the Greater, best version of ourselves that we share with Source energy and the universe, we can co-create heaven on earth.

Create a habit of waking up eager to start your day with light. You will be amazed at what a difference it makes and how much more positive you feel about your day ahead. All too often, a new day begins with the same *de-pressing* problems and concerns as the day before. The clock is ticking and a rush to check the email, get ready for work, "fight" traffic, and inevitably the heaviness of stress ensues.

Why not fill your mind with the positivity of *light*ness, with a *knowing* that you *are* creating what you are imagining.

Practice E

Imagining yourself as pure light

Remember ... As you imagine it, so are you creating it

1. Take several deeper, relaxing breaths as you imagine your spine like an empty pole being filled with light. Calling even more light to yourself, watch as it spreads out further and further into a sphere of light all around you.

2. You are formless and shapeless in this sphere of light, and you are safe and secure.

3. Imagine a path of light ahead of you representing your day.

4. See yourself doing everything you normally do as you touch others with your light. Picture whatever you anticipate doing during your day unfolding perfectly. Your emotions are calm and balanced. You have co-created your perfect day with a calm and balanced universe through your imagination.

You can create your future by filling it, day by day, with light.

As you wake up each morning, imagine filling yourself with light as you just did, and imagine a lit-up path of light ahead of you, creating harmony and balance throughout your day. And as you go to bed at night, appreciate all that occurred in perfect flow and harmony.

Little by little you can hold light and feel lighter as you imagine filling yourself each day with light. Remember light is powerful. Light is life itself! In our world, life would not be possible without the light coming from our sun. Light holds many gifts and can be used to better our lives, both physically and mentally!

You are evolving, becoming lighter and lighter, free of the baggage that once brought you down. You are moving forward to create your life in the way you want.

As you evolve in greater light you are learning to use your light to create a future that is perfectly balanced and flowing, everything working in harmony. Your thoughts and emotions are now future-oriented, no longer are you harboring the unwanted thoughts and emotions of the past that produced hardship and made you suffer. Nor are you harboring thoughts of a worst-case scenario of the future.

Sending light to your day ahead every morning will expand your light so that one year from today you are closer to en**light**-enment. Imagine you as your future self a year from today. Your mind is clearer, you are now more able to hear your inner guidance. You are wiser and more appreciative of all life. Your level of abundance has increased because it is now available from an infinite Universal Source, of which you are a part.

As you send light to your future self, your future self has reciprocated in kind by sending you light as well. Your future self is sending you the energy of wisdom and lessons, learned along your path of self-awareness.

A year from now, you are the higher consciousness of your future self. Your creativity is expanded. You feel limitless, free, and revitalized. You feel more joy, more peace, and more uncon-ditional love.

Merge with your future self, taking just seconds several times a day. Imagine a bridge of light going upward between you and your future self and picture the bridge dissolving in light, increasing your light as you merge and become your future self.

Can you call even more light to yourself? Can you immerse and saturate yourself in it and with it? Remember that light is infinite. There is no end to the light that can be brought into your life.

The light of consciousness knows only goodness and pureness, and you have been filled with pure goodness. Gone is the anxious stress, worry, regret, resentment, self-loathing, and disillusionment. You now feel peace, joy, and appreciation more often than ever. And you hold no judgment, no rancor because as a being of a higher consciousness you are not only indestructible, infinite, and everlasting, you are powerful perfection and beauty within.

Remember that pure, good feelings will bring into your reality your life, those things you want because good, high vibrational feelings reflect back everything that is good. Now those material things you have wanted, have a better chance of coming into your life.

Formless and selfless

Practice F

Become good at picturing the light in your center, imagining yourself shapeless and formless.

In the following practice:

Feel the true you, who you really are

1. Feel the peace as you imagine a wave of light coming in through the top of your head, saturating your whole body in peace and tranquility.

2. Put focus on slightly deeper, comfortable breaths until you feel calm. Notice the freedom of letting go.

3. The light within you has increased and you are now a sphere of light growing in strength and power and reaching out further and further.

4. Keep focusing on your breath and add awareness of feelings and sensations within your body. Do you have a relaxed and comfortable feeling somewhere in your body? Do you feel pain or discomfort anywhere in your body? Pay attention to the feeling of comfort or discomfort and notice that they dissolve on their own.

5. If a thought comes through, come back again and again to awareness of your breath and the sensations in your body and your sphere of light.

Much more is happening than you may realize as you do this practice. You are calming and settling thoughts and at the same time you are making space between them.

You are focusing on your formless self as you practice here. You are realizing your identity, the Self that is connected to an infinite universe.

It is far better to go within to the core of your being, the rich, safe, and secure spaciousness within you than to put your attention on what is happening "out there."

As you experience your formless Self through imagining yourself as pure light, you begin to understand you are much more than just the physical self that will come to an end in this physical existence. You are an infinite, ever-lasting Source Energy. You are realizing that as you bring focus and awareness to your formless self, you begin to know who you really are, your true identity. You are not the mortal self who is saddened by the past and worries about what the future holds. *Feeling and being* your formless Self allows you to let go and dissolve energies that once harmed you. You realize that you can be just as alive, and even more so, as you live aware of your formless Self in the restful consciousness of silence and non-thought.

The more you identify with your formless Self, the more you become "Self-less." This is the Self that looks at the outside world and wants to be helpful, because the "selfish" identity of the false ego has gradually fallen away.

You also become filled with light at your core. The word "core" means heart in Latin. As your heart and your whole (holy) being fills with light, unconditional love awakens within you for all life. There is nothing more you need. You are everything within. And nothing can be taken away. The power you have is not like the power we think of in the outer world. It is the power of knowing who you are and feeling at peace, whole and complete. You are beyond measure, and you know you are connected to an infinite Source Energy.

Know yourself as the radiant light that you are

You have a better understanding of how great and wonderful life can be when you are the master. You ascend toward higher consciousness not as somebody, but as nobody!

You really are *nobody* as you ascend toward higher consciousness, and that's beautiful because you have opened to an infinite spaciousness that changes every corner of your life!

As you imagine yourself formless and having nothing, you are in the rich spaciousness of the quantum field and the energy field of light, which are interrelated because each takes you to a space of an infinite source. This is the space of infinite possibilities and potentialities.

The connection to your higher, true self, and spirit is now more real.

The peaceful joy that you feel more and more often is what you have nurtured, cultivated, refined, and now express. You are the master of your life.

You no longer rely on the outside world to bring you happiness. You create your own peace, joy, love, and bliss in the world. And you are powerful.

And if something goes wrong in the outside world, you won't be joyful, but you **will** be at peace.

In every moment you are guiding your life in the direction you want. And it comes from an awareness of who you really are; a spiritual being who is part of a vast, unlimited universe, having a human experience.

CHAPTER FIVE

Creating Your Future

*Fall in love with your future, not with
your past.* —Dr. Joe Dispenza

ll too often we waste our energy by looking to past resentment, regret, or sadness rather than looking to the future with our highest desires and aspirations.

As you have awareness of your surroundings and of yourself within, you are allowing the low energies that used to be a major part of your life and that no longer serve you to dissolve naturally. Your focused, aware presence allows all negativity to simply fall away.

The Universal flow is positive, real, and true and does not recognize the past because the past has no relevance *now*. Remember that *life exists only in this moment*. You can only connect with the universal flow *now*.

As you go about your day be aware of where you are putting your attention. Are you focusing on problems or are you focused on imagining your future with enthusiasm?

Keep in mind that as you focus on the future you are reigning in and anchoring the mind that continually brings up the past.

No longer are you in the low energies of distracting, scattered thoughts that once ruled your life.

Little by little a life of greater joy, abundance, love, wisdom, creativity, and peace is unfolding. You have let go and you are free to create the life you want. A new vitality and energy follow, becoming your daily experience!

Thoughts create our reality

The thoughts we have had in the past have manifested the life we are experiencing today. Everything that surrounds us, we have created. Whether we think so or not, thoughts *do* create our reality. Every one of us has created our life through the thoughts we think and the emotions we feel.

Does it make sense that if you have created your life through your thoughts, could you not change your life through a new way of thinking, through new thoughts?

You are already aware of how being grateful and appreciative can improve your life through an open heart that is focused on good, elevated thoughts and feelings. Remember that being grateful and appreciative is the easiest, quickest way to feel free and let go moment by moment. Developing a habit of being appreciative improves every aspect of your life. You are more satisfied, changing your perspective on life. You increase self-love and even your health and well-being!

The good news is that you have already practiced a new way of thinking and feeling here. This makes it possible for you to bring about the life you've always wanted more quickly than if you had not yet practiced new ways of thinking and being.

You now understand that it is not just hoping, wishing, and longing for something to manifest and appear in your life. You now understand that a combination of the tools you've learned here will make real what you want in a much easier and effortless way. The tools you are learning here will allow low energies to fall away that no longer serve you.

As you practice allowing low energies like anger, regret, worry, and stress to fall away you are developing a muscle that will bring you endless gifts. Just as developing your muscles may be painful hard work at first, as you continue, you reap the rewards of the work you put in.

Practice pure relaxation

However, the "work" you are practicing here is pure relaxation as you align with the core and center of yourself where you are sowing seeds that will sprout unbelievable rewards in your life. It is a practice of being the person who deserves to live the life you've always wanted. It is expressing and being the higher true self that attracts everything needed because you are living the best version of yourself in pure, good, elevated thoughts.

Remember that as you live expressing higher, finer thoughts like appreciation and gratitude you open your heart and let go of judgment and unforgiveness. *And, with an open heart, your brain is benefiting because new neuropathways are being created so that the heart and the brain come together as one.* Now the brain that thinks is unified with the heart that *knows*. The connections to neurons in the brain will now help you transform into new ways of being, with new skills, and new memories. Your more orderly brain will now learn new skills more easily and bring about new, elevated, clearer memories.

The space beyond your everyday mind is the infinite spaciousness that changes your life for the better. It is the upward spiral of a higher consciousness that you are reaching moment by moment.

The path of mastering your life by falling in love with your future is magical!

CHAPTER SIX

Manifesting the Life You've Always Wanted

Whatever the mind can conceive and believe,
it can achieve. —Napoleon Hill

Allow yourself to picture your greatest desire in life. Go as big and "unlikely" as you want. Remember Universal Source has an infinity of gifts and rewards that are boundless and unlimited.

You can dream big. You are aligning with the Universal Mind that is constantly moving forward and evolving. You must evolve with it as you ask for all that is good and pure, always asking sincerely for something that does not violate anyone.

You are a co-creator with the universe

Can you remember a moment when you felt exhilarated and excited? Any moment that you can remember as a heightened enthusiasm and joy are experiences you can use to manifest something you want. Perhaps you were out with friends or on a family vacation and you felt enthused and joyous. Perhaps you were told something that made you so happy, so overjoyed, you can still taste and touch the feeling!

Your body will respond to a thought and an imagined future with an elevated feeling. Your brain and your body will now merge and align to create what you are thinking, imagining, and feeling.

Get very clear on what you want to manifest. Imagine it clearly using your five senses. Allow it to become real in your imagination. If there are people, you might picture someone saying something to you that gives you great joy.

Immerse yourself in the feeling of the person who already has whatever it is you want. Be that person.

Be the person that already has what you want

It is important to be and act the part, as if what you want you already have. In this way you are living the truth of what you want to see in your life. Be mindful of what you say and do, expressing wise thoughts.

Remember that bringing something that you want into your life requires that you experience *the feeling of already having what you want. Your imagination and the picture you put out must be clear. You must know with precise clarity what you want.*

Keep in mind that the brain and the subconscious do not know the difference between what you imagine, what you think and speak, and what is real. It does not discern. It takes everything in as truth.

Feel the excited emotion of what you want

Feeling the excited emotion of something that you want if you had it now is a very important step because feelings and emotions are what the body understands. This indicates to your body that it's real. Immerse yourself in the feeling. Let the feeling wash over you.

The energy you are immersing in and allowing to wash over you is the rich energy that brings you gifts and rewards. *Sincerely feel the electrical charge of physically living what you want.*

Remember that an important part of manifesting is the energetic "fuel" of a high vibration, like a good feeling to give to an energetic picture you have imagined of something you want. As you give fuel to the picture of what you want, you are adding a high vibrational frequency. Your strong emotional feeling gives it the power to become real and manifest.

A heightened, fired up feeling is at the core of manifestation!

Stay in positive energies

Staying with the energy that attracts gifts and rewards is crucial. Because once you have aligned your mind, body, and spirit, *any low energy* that does not align with a new infinite, indestructible energy you have tapped into, simply put, will not work.

As Neuroscientist, Dr. Joe Dispenza puts it, "You just got to stay there!"

The way to stay there in your elevated feelings that will manifest what you want is to appreciate and have gratitude throughout your day. Affirm that what you want is here now.

Appreciate life! Fill your day with positivity. Use the many tools you are being given here.

Create positive energy and the belief that what you want is here.

Become aware of signs, inspirational ideas, and insights

As you express and live more positively a higher number of thoughts become inspired ideas and insights. These ideas and insights are coming from the vast and infinite higher consciousness you are now reaching. Listen for the thoughts that inspire and act on them. A good idea may come from out of nowhere and could be the one that will take you to accomplish what you want. Be guided by your intuition.

Be assured that inspirational thoughts and insightful ideas will come through because your mind is clearer and no longer obstructed by useless noise. You have let go of the commotion coming from a mind that is incapable of offering you inspirational ideas and insights. The noisy, agitated mind is devoid of the energy of higher vibrational thoughts and has never offered you an inspirational insight. Not one!

Only when you are *aware in Presence*, can you receive signs and ideas that offer you solutions and answers that help move your life forward so that you can achieve your goals and aspirations. When you are present, heart-based, grounded, and balanced, you can access inspirational thoughts that fire-up and motivate you to take the action necessary to create the life you have always wanted.

Can you stay in the elevated energies, the elevated thoughts and feelings, of a higher consciousness that holds endless gifts and rewards for you? You are practicing doing that here.

Can you practice expressing higher thoughts and feelings in the next twenty-four to forty-eight hours? Remember that each time you go toward a higher quality of consciousness and more positive thoughts and feelings you are seeding seeds. It is as if you are removing the weeds of unwanted thoughts and cultivating the new growth of positive, finer, higher thoughts and feelings. Just as you are removing the weeds of unwanted thoughts and feelings, to grow a healthy blossoming plant, weeds must be removed and nutrient-rich soil maintained.

You may be thinking that it's not that easy for you to be positive in a world that is mostly not positive. Take little steps. Instead of aiming for twenty-four to forty-eight hours, aim for a couple of hours daily. Little by little you will get to a point where you can immerse yourself in the positivity of elevated thoughts and feelings for longer intervals. Remember that unwanted thoughts and their emotions that cause frustration, yearning, and impatience have no relevance to who you are becoming.

Do not wonder when or how something you want will make its appearance

Once you understand that without a shadow of a doubt you can manifest and attract gifts and rewards into your life, you will develop trust, and you will surrender, with no stress or anxiety, creating a life that is more effortless than ever.

More than ever, you are free, and you have let go, no longer feeling the chaos and pollution of an outer world.

You may ask Source energy for anything at all because you are an integral part of it. However, allow what you want to manifest and become real in your life to make its appearance in any way at all. It may not come as you imagined. The more you align with affirmed thoughts that turn into beliefs, the more you align with being appreciative, grateful, and present. And the more you align with being appreciative and present, the more the low energies of impatience or anger simply fall away.

There is no effort or hard work involved in letting go of low energies when you are living in the elevated, higher consciousness, focused on this moment, now.

Ask for something you want, imagine it, then let it go. It may come to you in a completely different way than you imagined. And that's okay! Appreciate and be grateful, no matter how it comes to you.

In the following chapter more will be said about thoughts that block and stop you from creating the life you've always wanted.

CHAPTER SEVEN

Letting Go of Negative Thinking

Keep your face always toward the sunshine and
shadows will fall behind you. —Walt Whitman

There is no doubt you are awakening, growing, and expanding toward higher consciousness moment by moment. However, even though you have more moments of realizing who you really are, at times, your experience of unwanted thoughts that are on autopilot resurface. The good news is that you really and truly *are* growing and expanding into higher consciousness despite the unwanted thoughts that resurface. However, it is not about getting from point A to point B. Higher consciousness is a journey that meanders and detours.

And there is much more going on than you may think.

Our daily life is riddled with things we must do to maintain our quality of life. The errands, the maintenance of our physical body, the meals, the conversations, the things that we perceive to go "wrong," the on-going events that are happening twenty-four hours a day and that are always changing, and not always for the better. We are more aware than ever that the continually changing aspect of the outer world cannot violate or disturb our innermost self.

Keep in mind that everything is an experience, whether good or bad. There is no judgment in consciousness, nothing is categorized as either one way or another. Since you are here to experience, why not make what you experience as positive and joyful as possible?

Having doubt about the joy and positivity you want to manifest in life completely stops it from becoming real. This is because doubtful thoughts and feelings you put out in the world attract the same low-level vibration. Remember that having elevated, higher vibrational thoughts is what you will experience through situations and circumstances; everything that just happens to you.

If you want to manifest something, everything completely stops if your thoughts are of a lower energy, frequency, and vibration like impatience and doubt: "When is it coming?" or "I don't think it will come."

The reason many give up on manifesting is because they go back to the same low energies of stress, anxiety, impatience and negative, fearful emotions that are considered a natural part of everyday life. No matter how much suffering these low energies cause, they simply feel familiar. Manifestation only works when there is trust and all doubt is released.

Absolute belief and knowing must replace doubt

Consider for a moment if you have any kind of doubt that creating a better future is real.

Perhaps there is fear of the unfamiliar, the unknown, and you would rather stay in what has always been familiar to you: listening to a mind that keeps you indulged in thoughts of the past or thoughts of worry of what the future may bring.

You are practicing here to become familiar with who you really are, your true authentic self. As you take deep breaths in relaxation and calming peace you are opening a path to living worry-free and less and less concerned with "problems."

As you commit to becoming familiar with a higher consciousness through the practice of just being and expressing a better, more elevated, Greater version of yourself you are little by little trusting that you can, indeed, create what is in your heart. And the more familiar you become with this state of consciousness, the better you can manifest and make real the life you've always wanted.

Perhaps you have a deep-seated belief that problems and concerns are natural and there is really no solution unless you try to control everything that happens.

You are not your negative thoughts

Remember that you are not your negative thoughts so that it is easy to dissolve thoughts coming from the everyday mind. These thoughts of no light hold no power at all. Anything that makes you feel bad, that doesn't bring light and high energy can be dissolved in an instant. Especially when you gain more and more light as you are practicing here.

Be creative in any way you choose to make a thought disappear, without battle or fight as you have practiced here.

Don't worry if unwanted thoughts that cause hardship make their appearance often. Keep in mind it is more important to bring the wandering mind back quickly to an elevated good feeling, than to worry about how often unwanted thoughts make their appearance.

Monitoring how you feel often is a good way to make your way back to a good feeling. Just as in meditative practice when you bring the wandering mind back again and again to your breath, throughout your day, you also bring your wandering mind back again and again to a good feeling.

Be creative in the way you dissolve unwanted thoughts. Allow unwanted emotions to pass through you as they dissolve in light, as you practiced earlier in this book. Affirm positive statements. Meditate by focusing on your breath and bringing focus back to your breath again and again.

As you bring focus back again and again to your breath, you are training your mind to become familiar with an awareness of the precious space that changes every corner of your life. You are not failing but *moving forward* no matter how many times you must come back again and again to a peaceful, good feeling. You are doing much more than you know. You are no longer a victim. You are the master of your life!

You now realize that the attitudes, opinions, and beliefs you hold that cause your mood to come down are the energies you attract, not allowing you to master the life that you want and deserve. You are a magnificent being!

You have everything within to create the life you want

You now understand that as you notice the cycle of worry about a fleeting issue in your life, it is like a wake-up call nudging you in the direction of creating your life through the vast spaciousness of infinite possibilities and potentials.

Your point of power is increasing, expanding your consciousness into higher light, wisdom, and unconditional love. The life force energies of a higher consciousness are infinite in nature and greater in power than thoughts or emotions coming from the everyday mind, making it easier to simply shift without effort to a better feeling.

There is much more that comes into your reality as you become aware of knowing and being who you are. Once you express and live the greater version of yourself, your true authentic self of higher consciousness, what may seem like miracles begin to appear.

Things you want now come to you effortlessly

You now notice that you appreciate life more often than ever. This alone will improve your life because you have opened your heart. Relationships improve as a result. Life flows in more harmonious ways. When you are aware of who you are moment by moment, there is no need to try to manifest whatever it is you want. Those things you want now make their appearance more effortless than ever.

As you take a relaxing peaceful breath now in this moment you are open and receptive. You can create from this space. As you look around at what you have already created, you can appreciate and be grateful. You are not judging whether it is good or bad, it is what it is. You know that little by little you are creating the life you've always wanted.

There is no need to struggle as you climb the upward spiral to a higher consciousness. You are aware in this moment and that is enough! Having awareness is the key. Remember, consciousness *is* awareness.

We make life much more complicated than it needs to be. There is nothing more you need to happen outside of yourself to bring you joy, peace, and growth. You have everything you need within. The change you want is here now, in this moment as you appreciate and have gratitude. Acknowledge and have compassion for how far you've come on your journey of awakening. Simply take a peaceful relaxing breath *now.*

We must not forget the sacred gift of the amazing engineering of our physical body that, when it is unencumbered and free of upsetting thoughts and emotions, maintains its perfect flow and well-being.

And the perfect flow continues through events, situations, and circumstances that just happen to us. So that the best of life, the life we've always wanted now comes to us easily and effortlessly.

Soon you will not have to be deliberate in finding a good feeling because the new neuropathways that are being created in your brain will help you easily hold the higher, finer thoughts of consciousness effortlessly without you having to be purposeful of what you say, think, and do.

Remember that you are the master of your life, creating the life you want no matter what is happening in the outer physical world.

The life that you want as you focus and imagine is real and true. You are creating it in the same moment you are imagining it. You are successful in this moment, now, as you put attention and focus on the creation of your life.

Remember consciousness is effortless!
Things you want now come to you effortlessly!

CHAPTER EIGHT

Awakening Peace in the World

Darkness cannot drive out darkness only light can do that
Hate cannot drive out hate, only love can do that.
—MartinLuther King

Much has been written about the darkness versus the light. However, darkness and light are not opposing forces. The Universal life force energies are peaceful and supportive. And the peaceful, Universal flow is within us. As the morning sun rises over the horizon, the light easily dissolves the darkness without fight or battle. And darkness allows the light to shine easily and effortlessly.

Just as light shows us the way in the outer world, we are practicing being the light that easily dissolves the darkness of hardship and suffering within, turning it into light. For once the darkness that no longer serves us dissolves in light, we create a brighter light, a brilliance of a higher energy, as we express thoughts and feelings of peace, compassion, and unconditional love.

We become a beacon of light, more able than ever to spread our luminous light further and further out to overcome the darkness of suffering and hardship in the world!

However, we can only become a beacon of light as we live in the light*er* energy of a higher consciousness. We attain a higher level of consciousness when we live deliberately focusing on good thoughts, deeds, and feelings, which eventually becomes a natural way of being. We take deeper breaths, always aware of expressing a higher level of wisdom and discernment. We can then send nourishing light to those in darkness who cannot feel light. Sending compassion and unconditional love to those who do not feel the beauty and bliss of the real and true energy that surrounds each of us.

If we can change and transform our everyday lives through a focus on positive, good, pure thoughts and feelings in as simple a way as taking deep comfortable, peaceful breaths, then why couldn't the outer world change and transform through the same positive goodness we emanate out to our personal outer world, changing circumstances and situations?

The truth is the outer world *can* also change! Each of us is a miniature but vital version of a dynamic Universal life force energy that we can use to change what we want to see in the world!

When we, the human collective, add to the evolving harmony and balance in the universe, the world at large we experience daily through the news and headlines will reflect the same.

It is crucial to understand that a focus on your Self within is more important than focusing and wondering about what is going on "out there."

You are a powerful contributor to peace in the world

As each of us goes within and finds peace we will **be the peace** we want to see in the world. We will then be a powerful contributor to peace in the world!

Each of us is a drop in the ocean of life with the power of the whole ocean. When we are at peace with what is happening daily in the outer world, when we are at peace with those who have different points of views from our own, change *will* come. And when we understand that no one must change for us; that it is us being at peace that changes everything, only then can everything in our world change.

> *The internal shift must happen*
> *before the external shift can be made*

The good news is that as hundreds of thousands make internal changes, there will begin an external change in the world we see.

Humanity is today experiencing an internal shift toward a higher consciousness of compassion, unconditional love, and wisdom. And this internal shift must happen before the external shift! The human collective is realizing more than ever the futility of war, a fight and battle that leads only to suffering and resolves nothing. Our own internal war of fighting the darkness is like a mirror projection of our external world.

Remember that we are a microcosm to the macrocosm of the universe. Everything within us mirrors the workings of the universe. So that we are its miniature version.

There are many moving parts to what happens in the outer world that none of us can control, just as there are many moving parts to everything we experience in our personal outer world. Why internalize situations and events that we cannot control that cause harm to our mental, emotional, and physical bodies?

Why internalize the turmoil going on in the headlines and what we see and hear on daily news? Why internalize fearful conversations? And why internalize the pollution of the outer world in the depths of the confusion of differing opinions and beliefs?

The good news is you are already learning to keep the pollution away as you bring back again and again a fearful, worried mind to your peaceful center within the pages of this book. This is a peaceful and effortless practice that allows, yet never resists or fights anything.

You are the watcher, witness, and observer of an outer world from a serene, peaceful, secure spaciousness within. You are the clear sky behind the stormy clouds that are transient and temporary. And you are the calm depth of the ocean and not the turbulence on the surface.

Think carefully if what you say and do is what you really want to see in the world! We have within us in every moment an ability to influence the world. In each moment you are resonating with the higher energy of peace and joy you have deliberately cultivated and now express!

You are the master and creator! *In any moment you can bring in the peace and joy we all deserve.* And believe it! It goes out limitlessly to a world that desperately needs your indestructible energy.

As you cultivate and express the higher energies of a higher consciousness you become a beacon of light for others, and you help heal a world that is in great need of healing.

However, there is a need to tread slowly and carefully. You have a new realization and understanding that you are a magnificent being of unconditional love and forgiveness. You are non-judgmental and free of any debilitating emotion that blocks your path of ascension to become and express the high-minded consciousness that you truly are.

Doesn't it make sense that non-judgment and unconditional love must include those that we believe have brought us great strife in the outer world? You might believe that our world would be better off without those that seem to be the cause of suffering.

We are given the opportunity to be better, to come together as one, and to have great compassion for all, no matter what their deeds are. We humans can then awaken to ascend and find our true moral heights.

You as a creator can imagine the future you want and the future you want to see in the world. As you picture a better world, there is forgiveness of those you may hold accountable for the challenges in the world.

You can create the world you want to see

Practice G

In the following practice create a vision of peace in the world:

Imagining the world you want to see

Take a few deep breaths until you are at peace within. Picture a scene in which hundreds of thousands of people are gathered in silence. As you envision a world you would like to see, everyone showing each other appreciation, respect, and love, imagine that each person is envisioning the same peaceful world that you see. Make it real by adding the joy you feel in the realization that humanity is finally coming together as one in peace, and finally, in love.

Remember, as you imagine it so are you creating it.

You are unconditional love, peace, and joy and one with all life and all of humanity no matter what is done or how it is acted out in this earth life experience we share.

Going against and battling with who we perceive to be the one who is the cause of our suffering is not aligning with Source, of which we are a part. We have within us all the higher qualities of consciousness as Source Energy.

We may like to believe that the bad deeds of others will somehow justifiably get paid.

But we must be careful. We are unconditional love and light, at least that is what we are practicing daily, right?

Focusing on anger and worry is wasting a moment in time to be the creator of life. We cannot control an outer world simply through focusing on its problems. Just as we now understand that we don't try to control the situations and challenges in our own personal experience.

Simply taking a deep deliberate breath with intention amid a world filled with the commotion of polarities and dualities opens you to pure goodness that can permeate through every corner of life.

Humanity is awakening to a realization that there is no separation between everything and everyone in the universe. Each of us is in crucial need of this understanding because this alone could stop all wars, all hatred, discord, and barriers between people. There would be no reason for fences, for borders, or trespassing signs. It is crucial that the realization comes that when something is done to another it is done to each of us because we and all life are One.

Awakening to your Magnificence

Putting attention on inner peace, joy, and unconditional love that we are now much better at *being* day to day as the Greater version of ourselves, our true authentic self, is something we do daily, knowing that it is one of the most important things to do in life. Each of us can be a force of power as we emit and put out into the world our unique high vibrational energy of positivity and goodwill.

Stay focused on the truth of who you are, with attention on the energies within, and you will reap amazing results in your daily experience! As you practice peace, joy, and unconditional love for all you are seeding rewards in your relationships, circumstances, situations, and even extending peace out into the world! Because we are all connected as one, you alone are slowly but surely sprouting and creating milder, more beautiful experiences in your life and including the world at large!

When you see or think of those at the center of problematic situations in the world, send them compassion because they cannot feel love. Feel the freedom of letting go because the energy of compassion opens the heart and is a link to love.

Just as we experience growth in our personal lives through problematic challenges, the *human collective* is also experiencing an expansion of consciousness and growth through the problems and challenges that are plaguing our world. The higher quality of compassion is being expressed around the world by millions that are feeling this high vibrational energy that links the heart to love.

The feeling of compassion is the part you have, no matter how small you may think it is, to change a world that needs your conscious, aware injection, even if it comes from an inner feeling. A feeling is energy and goes out into the environment just as easily as a thought.

You become accepting enough to see the bigger picture of whatever those that do not think like you have experienced—what they have experienced in life that does not allow the flow of pure goodness and joy to come to the surface to be expressed.

Can you feel compassion for someone that cannot feel the beauty that truly exists in the world? Can you feel unconditional love no matter what another says or does?

As we live expressing our Greater self, we mirror higher consciousness. We do not judge, nor do we condemn and fight the forces we believe to be the cause of hardship. Instead, we put out the energies of compassion and love toward those that need love the most in the world.

Keep in mind that we cannot change the outer world through thinking and feeling angry and voicing opposition. An outer world can only change through the wisdom of a higher consciousness. It cannot change through the same low energy of anger and hate that produced the anger and the hate.

Forgiving those that we blame and hold responsible for our suffering is not something that comes easy to us. Everything negative we have ever experienced has seemed to lead us toward the path of resistance which is fighting and battling.

Humanity has been fighting, battling, and warring for eons. Using the same energy to try to solve a problem has never worked.

While we humans have been programmed to solve a problem by fighting and hitting back, only a higher, wiser consciousness can solve a problem.

When you care enough to know how you feel in each moment, that is when you grow in leaps and bounds. As you connect with the Universal Life Force energies you are transformed. And once you change—your perspective, how you look at life, how you treat yourself and others—to a better-quality of mind of a higher consciousness, that is when your outer world also transforms. Be assured, however, there's nothing much to do but remember to be aware of how you feel, always following with a deep breath to maintain your peace within. When you are at peace you are no longer angry, revengeful, or fearful.

We are powerful when engaged in the positive power of the Universe. Finding our balance and harmony is like the singer, pianist, and saxophonist attuning and creating the harmonic flow of beautiful sounds, the weaver who brings together the threads to create a lovely tapestry, and the visual artist who creates through stunningly gorgeous strokes. This is the beauty we innately know that resonates with the flowing harmony of an infinite Universe.

We are here to maintain harmony and balance as Source Energy in the state of a higher, wiser consciousness.

The world will change through the universal energies that are pure, good, upright, virtuous, and noble. The world will not change simply through man's laws because they can be broken.

Remember that Universal laws are stable, unwavering, indestructible, and infinite.

It is a beautiful time to be alive because as humanity feels the powerful shifts from darkness to light, we are each gaining the power to change the world. We live in an amazing cosmos filled with energies that can be tapped to better the quality of our lives. As the quality of our personal life improves, those around us will "catch" our more vibrant alive energy.

We have a birthright to the infinite, vibrational frequencies that lead to the creation of the life we have always wanted. Compassion and, finally, love unfold as we want to help.

As you practice here, your mind is more peaceful. Your physical body is calmer. You are an observer of life, not getting involved in it. You are allowing things to be just as they are, not trying to control anything. You are protecting your sacred, infinite, indestructible innermost being from the pollution of an outer world. And you are the master of your life, no longer relying on something out there to make you happy!

These are the steppingstones, the guideposts, to an expression of the best version of the Self. This is the journey of truth that you are taking as you learn to maneuver this third dimensional existence so that you can come home to Source Energy and free yourself of the suffering of a conflicted, complicated world. As you attune to Source Energy, you can live in your heaven on earth, despite what is happening in the outer world.

If we as a collective can feel compassion toward one another on the other side of the world, we can extend that compassion linked to love to our local communities, neighborhoods, friends, and loved ones. It is good enough as you simply think the thought of wanting to help your fellow human beings. The energy of thoughts of a desire to help goes out into the environment in a more powerful way than you might think. You can help a world in crisis simply through your intentional good thoughts and feelings. Remember that good intentions go beyond actions taken.

Love is the highest vibrational energy

You are getting to know who you are as the higher consciousness, and you are realizing that everyone is interconnected. Each human being is a precious Source Energy. You would never think to harm another because harming another is harming yourself.

At times you may wonder how you can help a world in jeopardy. You might think there is absolutely nothing you can do because whatever is happening out there looks hopeless.

When you feel so good, so much joy and bliss, you want it for others. However, you may still wonder how to help others live life with more peace and less struggle.

Remember to do the "Imagining the world you want to see" practice that you did earlier in this chapter, because as you imagine it so are you creating it.

Know that in this moment you can emanate the highest vibrational energy of love. This unbelievable force can go out into the environment influencing all energies. You are emanating the highest energy, and you are free, and you have let go. You are at peace, calm, and you are love itself, spreading love as it goes out further and further and coming back to you, reflecting the energy of love into your life in endless ways.

From this elevated state, you can also create a symbol that represents peace and love. Symbols are easy to imagine in the space of a quick moment. You can imagine a symbol you have created going out to a world in need of the energies of peace and healing. You might add a luminous light to your symbol that goes out, encircling the world.

You can help either a friend or loved one, or the human collective by "holding space" for them. You can do this by elevating your energy to the highest energy of love. Remember that maintaining the energy of appreciation and gratitude is an effective way to activate the elevated energy of love because your heart opens when you are appreciative and grateful.

You can then hold space by imagining the person or the human collective you are sending energy to, as living the life they have always wanted. See them expressing peaceful calm and joy, hearing them say something meaningful about their life.

Perhaps they are expressing how their life has changed because they now know what really matters.

As you imagine holding space for those you hold accountable for misdeeds done in the world or to yourself, you are free. It is as if you have cleansed yourself of the harmful energies of anger and unforgiveness. And you can hold space with heads of states in the world with whom you hold differing viewpoints or with a loved one. There is no need to try hard or use effort. You do it easily without rancor or hard feelings. There is only forgiveness and a peaceful feeling.

This is how you and the world can heal.

You as part of the whole are important because you have the infinite power of the whole. You can do more in this very moment through a wiser, more peaceful, higher consciousness than you could ever do in a lifetime of physical work like marching in protest and holding signs and placards. That tells you how powerful you are and how important it is to elevate your energy toward a higher consciousness.

This is the beauty in the world today that seems so chaotic and difficult yet can heal through peaceful loving kindness. *It is the peace within us that gives peace to the world.*

Easy Access to Practices

Letting go and freeing yourself

Practice A

In the following practice you will experience your breath, the doorway into a spaciousness within that helps you let go and feel free.

Focusing on your breath to feel free and let go:
1. Take several comfortable, even breaths giving attention to both your breath and the relaxed, calm feeling of your physical body.
2. Put your feet and legs in a comfortable position as you relax your thighs and your hips.
3. Focus on your stomach, your shoulders, and neck breathing smoothly and evenly, relaxing even further.
4. Continue with slightly deeper breaths as you relax your head, the muscles around your eyes, and your mouth, dropping your jaw just a little.
5. If your mind wanders, bring it back again and again to a focus on your breathing and a focus on the peace you feel in your physical body.

Can you feel the peace and stillness as you relax your body, mind, and spirit?

You might think of your breath as a golden key that unlocks the door to many gifts and rewards in life.

Dissolving inner conflict

Practice B

All fear, tension, anger, and sadness, any inner conflict can vanish into nothingness as you imagine inner conflict dissolved in light. However, you need to be persistent in using light to dissolve thoughts. Because the more you fight, battle, and resist the low energies of unwanted thoughts, the stronger they become. So that as you *persistently imagine* dissolving thoughts easily and effortlessly with light, they will *exist only as light,* no longer harming you mentally and physically.

In the following practice imagine a powerful ray of light dissolving thoughts of worry, stress, tension, any inner conflict:

1. **Take several relaxing breaths until you feel peace and tranquility from your head to your toes.**

2. **Imagine a ray of light coming from a Universal sun that illuminates many worlds with its powerful rays. It is a golden light that cleanses and heals. Imagine it coming in through the top of your head.**

3. **As you take a comfortable breath in, allow the golden light to clear all energies in your body that cause you to suffer, holding your breath for a couple of seconds.**

4. **Then breathe out as if through a straw, slowly and comfortably, as you watch unwanted thoughts dissolve in light.**

5. Continue breathing in the golden light and breathing out unwanted thoughts until you feel calm.

Remember to be persistent in dissolving unwanted thoughts so that they *exist only as light.*

Merging your heart and mind

Practice C

In the following practice, your brain is absorbing the good and pure qualities of the heart.

Take slightly deeper, relaxing breaths so that you feel peaceful serene tranquility that extends from the top of your head to your toes. Continue until you feel completely relaxed. Put focused awareness on the area of your heart, imagining light pouring out from it. Imagine a stream of light coming from your heart extending upward to your mind and back downward to your heart. As you relax more deeply, imagine the stream of light extending upward, then downward to your heart again and again. Stay here as long as you like, feeling the peaceful tranquility and cohesion of your heart and mind, in harmony as one.

As you continue to focus on your heart, the energy field of love expands reaching all areas of your body, and out further and further, creating a sphere of light, reaching everyone and all life around you and beyond.

Remember that you have let go and are free as you revel in the peace and tranquility of an open heart, and you are perfect just as you are.

Dissolving unwanted emotions

Practice D

In the following practice, you are allowing a strong emotion to pass through you with no fight or battle:

Allow a low feeling of sadness, tension, or anger to pass through you
Take several deep, relaxing breaths and allow the *feeling, not the thought*, of a strong emotion to pass through the area of your heart. Feel the energy of the emotion no matter how intense. It is alright if you tear up, it is simply the strength of the emotion making its way through you. Imagine the emotion turning into light, dissolving within you. Continue focusing on the light within you as you take slightly deeper breaths feeling the serene tranquility of peace and calm. And imagine the light within you increasing in power and strength.

Eventually these strong emotional energies will subside, dissolving altogether, never to bother you again so that you can feel the freedom and the letting go.

Remember to think of the unwanted thought for just seconds, allowing only the energy of the emotion to pass through you.

Touching others with light

Practice E

Imagining yourself as pure light

Remember ... As you imagine it, so are you creating it

1. Take several deeper, relaxing breaths as you imagine your spine like an empty pole being filled with light. Calling even more light to yourself, watch as it spreads out further and further into a sphere of light all around you.

2. You are formless and shapeless in this sphere of light, and you are safe and secure.

3. Imagine a path of light ahead of you representing your day.

4. See yourself doing everything you normally do as you touch others with your light. Picture whatever you anticipate doing during your day unfolding perfectly. Your emotions are calm and balanced. You have co-created your perfect day with a calm and balanced universe through your imagination.

You can create your future by filling it, day by day, with light.

As you wake up each morning, imagine filling yourself with light as you just did, and imagine a lit-up path of light ahead of you, creating harmony and balance throughout your day. And as you go to bed at night, appreciate all that occurred in perfect flow and harmony.

Formless and selfless

Practice F

Become good at picturing the light in your center, imagining yourself shapeless and formless.

In the following practice:

Feel the true you, who you really are

1. **Feel the peace as you imagine a wave of light coming in through the top of your head, saturating your whole body in peace and tranquility.**

2. **Put focus on slightly deeper, comfortable breaths until you feel calm. Notice the freedom of letting go.**

3. **The light within you has increased and you are now a sphere of light growing in strength and power and reaching out further and further.**

4. **Keep focusing on your breath and add awareness of feelings and sensations within your body. Do you have a relaxed and comfortable feeling somewhere in your body? Do you feel pain or discomfort anywhere in your body? Pay attention to the feeling of comfort or discomfort and notice that they dissolve on their own.**

5. **If a thought comes through, come back again and again to awareness of your breath and the sensations in your body and your sphere of light.**

Much more is happening than you may realize as you do this practice. You are calming and settling thoughts and at the same time you are making space between them.

You are focusing on your formless self as you practice here. You are realizing your identity, the Self that is connected to an infinite universe.

Help manifest peace in the world

Practice G

In the following practice create a vision of peace in the world:

Imagining the world you want to see

Take a few deep breaths until you are at peace within. Picture a scene in which hundreds of thousands of people are gathered in silence. As you envision a world you would like to see, everyone showing each other appreciation, respect, and love, imagine that each person is envisioning the same peaceful world that you see. Make it real by adding the joy you feel in the realization that humanity is finally coming together as one in peace, and finally, in love.

Remember, as you imagine it so are you creating it.

Can You Please Help?

Please leave a helpful review. You would be helping this book spread the urgent human need of higher consciousness around the globe leading to peace in the world.

About the Author

Darla Luz is an award-winning writer who is passionate about increasing the evolution of human consciousness throughout the world by writing about it in an easy-to-understand way. She lives what she has written in this book. Most days are spent fulfilling her life's work as an on-going student of Consciousness so that she can help others live consciously aware in presence, free from struggle and inner conflict. She enjoys taking nature walks with her family observing the wilderness along the riverbanks and lakesides near her home.

www.ingramcontent.com/pod-product-compliance
Lightning Source LLC
Chambersburg PA
CBHW071611040426
42452CB00008B/1315